A WEEKEND WITH MATISSE

A WEEKEND WITH
MATISSE

By Florian Rodari
Translated by Joan Knight

Rizzoli
NEW YORK

H. Matisse Juill. 47

Voila! Barely ten o'clock in the morning and here we are well above the clouds on our way to Nice. I love the south of France and I know you will, too. I'm looking forward to our weekend together. I can't wait to show you where I live and work. In less than an hour you will see the Mediterranean, the harbor with its boats and white houses, and, as we land, the beautiful green trees and colorful flowers of Nice. It all makes me eager to get back into my studio and resume my work! You'll see where I live: in a lovely villa on a hill, filled with large rooms which I have furnished to my taste. I enjoy my privacy; the gardens that surround the villa protect me from prying eyes. Since I don't like to be disturbed, I have given my address only to a few close friends. Sometimes, I pin a card to the door, to let them know that they have in fact reached the villa of

HENRI MATISSE
artist painter

It's amazing, isn't it? A short hour ago, we were standing in the rain, in the middle of a traffic jam in Paris, our ears assaulted by the angry insults of motorists, our toes threatened by squealing tires. . . . Now we're above it all, as calm as can be, floating free in the blue light of limitless space. Isn't air travel miraculous? With a burst of speed, the engines lifted our plane off the ground and immediately our day-to-day worries fell away. The thoughts that fill our heads when we are earthbound appear trivial and small from up here. If I were a doctor, I wouldn't hesitate to prescribe air travel as an antidote for the weary and the worried!

As you can see, I am an old man now. I haven't been well lately and can be on my feet no more than a few hours a day. But today is an exception for me because of our adventure. Normally, I would be confined to a chair or my bed, across which I have installed a work table so that I may draw, paint, make collages...and even sculpt! I have lost the wonderful agility of youth and can no longer leap, dive, run, or swim as you do. On the other hand, simply by closing my eyes, I can release the powers of my imagination and, when I do, it takes me on the most amazing voyages, enabling me to dance with abandon and soar through space in ways that no athlete, even the most gifted and highly-trained, could ever imagine. . .

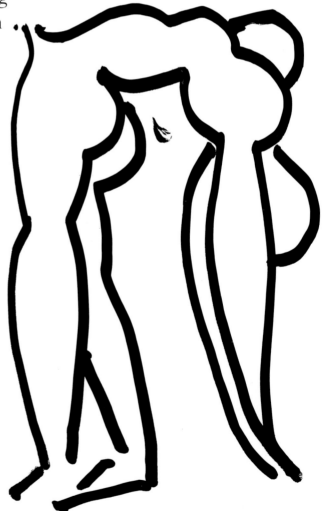

And so, in many of my paintings, I have set people free from the earth. My figures soar like birds or airplanes: dancers, first, who, through their movements, try to make their bodies lighter, more buoyant, echoing the arabesques of the music. Then acrobats, who bend and leap with such elasticity that they give the impression of effortless and perpetual motion.

A wealthy Russian merchant commissioned Matisse to paint this large canvas, Dance. *It was to hang in his house in Moscow, next to its companion piece,* Music.

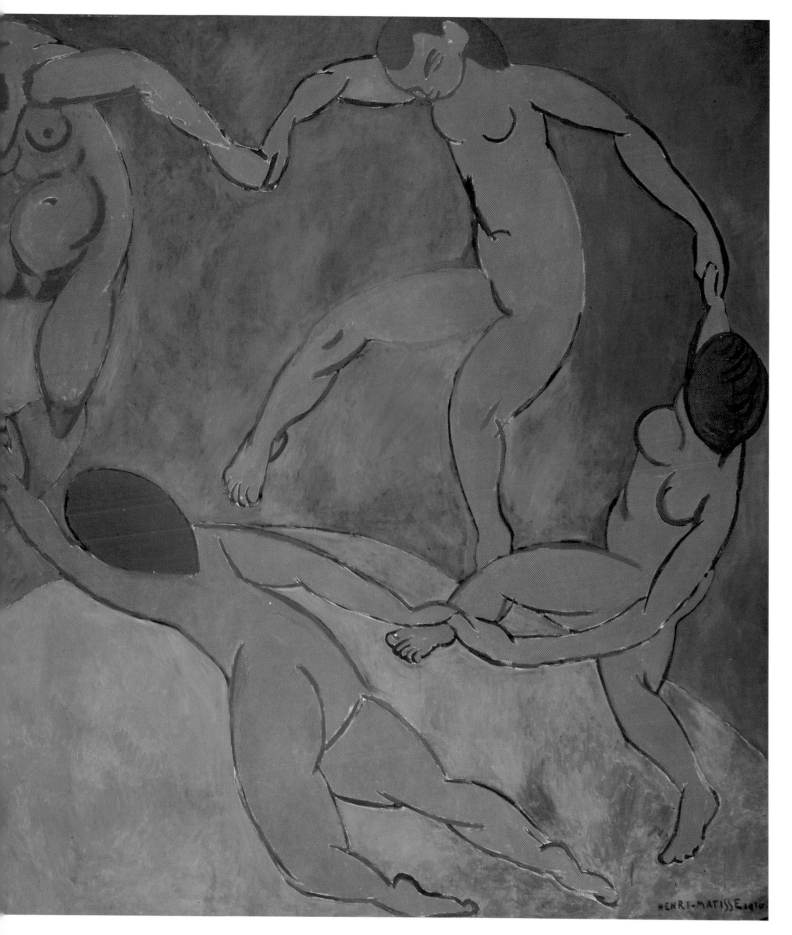

What lengths artists must go to in order to master the illusion of weightlessness! Hours of rehearsal before a performance is just right, buckets of perspiration to achieve a few seconds of perfect balance. All too often we forget that the momentary magic artists bring to us, whether they're acrobats, dancers, or painters, represents hours of relentless work, day after day, much like musicians who must endlessly practice their scales in the solitude of their training.

It's no different for me, when I paint or draw. To make an image that looks spontaneous on paper or canvas, I first have to observe the model I have chosen for a very long time and from every angle. Say it was you, *mon ami!* I would observe you for many hours before I could even start to do your portrait. First, we might play together, have a conversation, go for a stroll. Then, when I had discovered your favorite and most natural expression—and only then—would we undertake a sitting. You would have to be very patient. I would begin by sketching you over and over again to limber up my hand, to familiarize myself

with the features of your face; at first, the drawing would be precise, and look very much like you, but little by little I would worry less about capturing your likeness. Gradually, over a period of days, weeks, even months, I would content myself with a few features distinctive to your face—your mouth, your forehead, perhaps an ear. In the end, my pencil would guide itself. . . I could draw you with my eyes closed!

Five drawings of Jackie, Matisse's granddaughter.

H matisse 44

There! We're approaching Nice! Let's fasten our seat belts; we'll be landing in a few minutes. You know, I settled here nearly thirty-five years ago. I was probably drawn to it because it's so different from the north of France where I was born—a grim, dark region where the rain never stops falling on monotonous fields of beets. Here, at the edge of the Mediterranean, with its dazzling light and sun, I have found the quality of life and brightness of color that I need for my work.

The light! Ah, the light! It makes one feel so good and helps chase away dark thoughts. Earth tones, grays, and muddy browns are the colors of the painters of the north. Here, the sky above is blue and all around us are bright and joyful colors: the reds, greens, and yellows of flowers, trees, and the sunshine which warms our hearts and bodies.

Here we are at last. I'm so happy to be back at Villa Le Rêve. I have named my villa "The Dream" because I want everyone who comes here to feel as though they have entered a dream land and left their personal cares at the door. There are enough reasons to feel sad in today's world, you see. So, whenever I have the opportunity to do so, I create an atmosphere of happiness in my life and on my canvases—a kind of perpetual summer. Oh, I don't mean to say that I ignore suffering. Like everyone, I have experienced it on more than one occasion: with my countrymen during times of war, with my family when we had no money, and within my own body after having a serious operation.

But each time I chose not to dwell on it and I never let it into my heart. . . . No doubt one of the most flattering compliments one could ever pay me would be to tell me that my paintings bring comfort and a smile to the lips of those who gaze upon them.

Come with me into the garden: here, I have tried to recreate Paradise as it surely might have been. Flowers, trees, birds, and all sorts of wonderful creatures live in harmony here. Now let me show you the villa itself. Do you see how I have arranged things so that the inside and the outside spaces flow together? The garden spills over into the house, and the open windows, the murmur of the sea, the sigh of the wind, the perfume of the flowers, and the singing of birds combine to bring the outdoors in. In order to erase the boundaries still further, I had an enormous birdcage built and filled it with hundreds of birds. And, in this room, *voilà!* . . . a forest of exotic plants. This way, I have made sure there is always springtime at Villa Le Rêve—even during our few weeks of winter!

Be careful! This room is very cluttered, so watch your step! Take care not to knock over that precious vase or step on any of the fabrics. You see, like all painters, I collect odds and ends, which I take down from the cupboard when the mood strikes me and I feel like including them in my paintings.

Moroccan pottery, old coffeepots, dented trays, baskets filled with slowly-rotting fruits, armchairs and knick-knacks all reappear from time to time in my paintings. I set them up, like an army of toy soldiers, on a table or arrange them elsewhere in a room in a way that pleases my eye. Only I am allowed to touch these objects. Once I have used them, I send them back into the darkness of the cupboard for a few more years. Slowly they will gather dust, until I summon them back into service. They exist solely for the art of painting, and they know it.

My most deeply rooted passion, however, is my fabrics. See these cupboards? They're full of them. As I traveled around the world, I bought blankets, shawls, scarves, and dresses for my models to wear, as well as tablecloths, folding screens, rolls of colorful paper, and carpets which I tossed on the floor or hung on the walls in order to multiply the colors around me.

I did not buy these beautiful materials because of their usefulness, but rather for their designs which make my paintings more lively and gay. An ordinary carpet is for walking on, but a Persian carpet, richly woven, is an invitation to dream, to wander in the design of its arabesques. A carpet as beautiful as the one you see here on the left is a magical garden, a paradise in which your gaze will surely be lost if you try to follow its rich pattern of arches, flowers, and interlacings. Perhaps it is because these carpets transport the beholder's imagination to such faraway places that they are called "flying carpets" in tales from the Orient.

   Throughout his long life as an artist Matisse used many models, upon whom he imposed exhausting sittings, often without taking into account the fact that these young women might have a life of their own outside the world of painting, or that a lover might be waiting impatiently for them at the door for hours on end . . . He clothed them in sumptuous finery: colorful bodices, delicately embroidered shawls, skirts with bright stripes and revealing blouses, which he brought back from his travels or received from friends. The most regal costume ever worn by one of his models was no doubt this splendid dress, an expanse of blue with a flounce: light, diaphanous, trimmed with frothy white, the dress looks elegant against the black tiles of the room. The sitting for this portrait lasted several months, which was not unusual at all for Matisse.

For as long as I can remember, my eye has been drawn to the motifs of the decorative and folk arts. For me, the rhythmic repetition of similar shapes or colors in these arts weaves the same spell as a flower-filled meadow or the cresting of waves at sea. In the past, when painters painted a room, their intent was to draw the viewer into it. In my paintings, on the other hand, everything stays right on the surface: people, furniture, objects, a wall, a ceiling, and sometimes even the landscape outside the window, are all kept on the same plane. I don't use perspective or measure proportions with a ruler. Shading and modeling disappear; color and color alone defines the images on my canvas. Of course, you would not be comfortable in an interior of mine. Imagine yourself in this painting! It would be confusing to find yourself in a room where the only separation between the table and the wall is a thin black line and where the objects all look as though they could tumble onto the floor at any moment. A painting is not a box, it's a flat surface. And if I can make that surface sing, why, that's enough for me! But looking at the fruit on the table has made me hungry. Will you join me in the garden for lunch?

There are several reasons for Matisse's fascination with Oriental art and its influence on his painting: in 1909, he attended an exposition in Munich, Germany, where he admired Islamic ceramics, like the horse on the left and the pitcher, below, as well as Persian miniatures. Several months later, he went to Morocco and fell under the spell of the intense light and the brilliance of the fabrics. Then, invited to Moscow by Schukin, a wealthy collector who had bought many of his paintings over the years, Matisse visited Russian churches and discovered their simple designs and bold colors, as in this reproduction of St. George and the Dragon. This taught him that the art of the Orient was not concerned with duplicating everyday life and that, furthermore, in the works of Islamic and Russian artists, it is never five o'clock in the afternoon as it is in Impressionist paintings! In these works, pure colors invalidate time. Shadows are erased and forms are reduced to simple symbols that are repeated over and over again like notes of music.

The sun is so strong in Morocco that even black can function as color. In this painting, The Moroccans, *it becomes synonymous with blinding light. Here, the Moroccans, at left, bent over in prayer, are reduced to rhythmic forms that have very little to do with real people. They play a purely decorative role and contribute to the overall harmony of the painting, as do the flowers on the balcony and the dome beyond.*

Under the influence of the art of the Orient, Henri Matisse's palette took on more vivid tonalities than ever before. There was now a preponderance of blue, which never left; we find it in the paper cut-outs he created at the very end of his life. It's the blue of the Moroccan light, which bathes the city and its inhabitants, the blue of the clothing with which the Tuaregs (nomads of the central and western Sahara) envelope themselves, the blue of the mosaics which cover the domes of the mosques to give them buoyancy against a tranquil sky, as in the dome at the mausoleum of the Tartar conqueror, Tamerlane, on the opposite page.

But I rarely paint with brushes anymore. I work with cut paper instead. Yes, exactly, with scissors and paste! Child's play, my friends tease. . . . A dignified, distinguished old man like myself making cut-outs all day, that's not serious business!

Let them say what they may, they do not understand. Because, in truth, it really doesn't matter a bit which medium I use to reach my goal, just as long as my work stands on its own and I feel happy doing it. The technique I use for cut papers is really very simple. First of all, I cover large sheets of paper with bright colors: beautiful blues, deep greens, brilliant yellows, and so on. I have my assistant do this—it would tire me too much to do it myself. When I have a good stack set aside, I choose one sheet of paper and begin cutting out shapes with my large scissors. How much energy and time this saves me! No longer do I have to draw a figure and then color it with a brush! Because now I paint with my scissors and paste: I cut directly into color, like a sculptor carving a block of stone. Next, I gather up the pieces I will use to compose my figure. These I either paste onto a white sheet of paper or pin to the wall. Naturally, I have to know what I want to make well before I start out. But I think about it so much in advance that, by the time I begin, the thoughts are in my fingers and my scissors seem to conjure up shapes on their own. The experience is *extraordinaire,* my young friend: painting and sculpting had become difficult for me because of my ill health. The idea of using cut paper came to me in a flash when I was bored one night, and its effect has been miraculous: at my advanced age, I am still able to make beautiful works on a monumental scale.

I get so carried away with cut papers that the process takes on a life of its own: it's bigger than I am and I find myself surpassing by far the usual limits of painting. The canvas resting on its easel is no longer large enough, and soon even my room seems confining. My scissors lead me on; the designs that result multiply at my fingertips and spread over the walls like the leaves of some tropical plant growing out of control. Soon, I'll have to return to my studio in town. There I have many rooms and the ceilings are high enough to contain this new vegetation that flowers in my imagination. Perhaps I can show it to you this weekend. It's on the third floor of the Regina Hotel, a palatial building built in 1896 where Queen Victoria went for the winter holidays.

From that time on, the walls of Matisse's apartments were covered with enormous cut-paper compositions filled with exotic plant and marine life. If you look at them closely, you will see an amphibious world in which fish can be mistaken for birds, mermaids rub shoulders with parakeets, flowers look like animals, and animals like flowers.

Where do all these strange shapes come from, you ask? I'll tell you: twenty years ago, I embarked on a long voyage to the South Pacific. After a stop in New York, where I was impressed by the extraordinary lightness of the skyscrapers, I went to Tahiti and the neighboring islands. But when I got there, I found that the lazy life under the coconut palms, surrounded by pure, intense light and luxuriant vegetation, not to mention natives with voluptuous bodies, quickly grew boring and tiresome. Believe it or not, I could hardly wait to leave that tropical paradise and return to Paris! But I did have to wait for the boat to Europe and, while I did, I passed the days swimming in the clear waters of the lagoons. I barely drew a thing and, although I had expected to be very productive there, I came back from the voyage with no more than three or four drawings. What's more, years passed before I thought about the place again. But lately, my impressions of Tahiti, buried for so long, have been coming to the surface. Memory is an odd thing—it's always there, working inside us, even though we may not be aware of it!

And so it's taken years for my impressions of Tahiti to crystallize. What is now emerging blossoms at my fingertips. It is the essence of tropical life, filtered through time: fantastical fish, coral the color of blood, starfish, palms bent by the wind, chattering parrots, sinuous swimmers, green water under a golden sun, emerald seas, and skies so blue as to seem weightless and eternal.

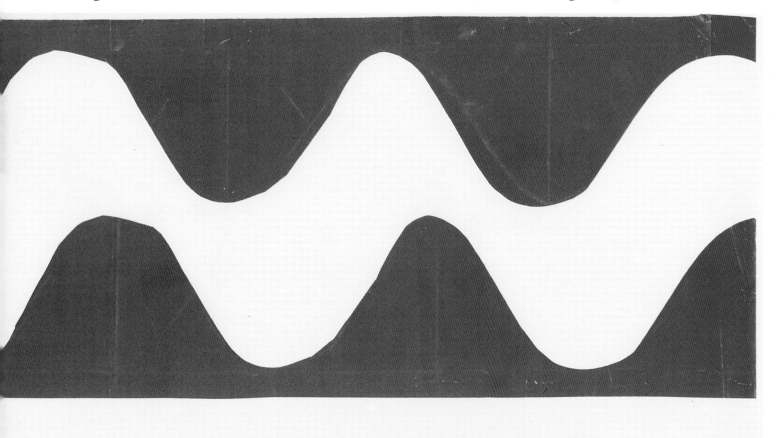

The brilliant light of the tropics remembered by Matisse is the same light he recaptured in a major undertaking begun in 1948—when he was nearly 80 years old! Not far from Villa Le Rêve, on a hillside facing the village of Vence, Dominican nuns planned to build a small chapel and they needed designs for the stained-glass windows. They turned to the master for advice.

Matisse was instantly enthusiastic about the chapel. No sooner had he begun work on the windows than he felt awaken within himself sensations of ten years before when, as an expert swimmer, he would dive down into the waters of the lagoon with his eyes open and resurface into the brilliance of the Tahitian sun. Matisse would bring the same feelings of joy and exhilaration to the chapel, creating a place where people could feel rested and happy. The intense greens, blues, and yellows of the windows throw pools of colored light onto the white marble floor and bring an airy quality to the interior of the chapel, which seems to float in a light of liquid gold. The project so caught Matisse's imagination that he went on, after the windows, to design every detail of the chapel, including the beautiful vestments worn by the priests.

But the day wears on. . . . Now, it's time for our *sieste.* The heat outside is overwhelming and the drone of the cicadas makes our eyelids heavy. This is my favorite time of day: inside the house, where it's still cool, some sleep, while others read, play quietly, or simply dream. Silence surrounds us and we live inside it. I have often evoked these moments of calm in my paintings, moments of reflection in which one's spirit gradually perceives subtle relationships between things, a kind of unseen harmony between form and color which causes them to resonate. One of my earlier paintings suggests this: in a room sheltered from the harsh sunlight and noise of the outdoors sits an open case containing my violin. There is no musician and yet we are aware of musical harmonies. There was no need for me to show the virtuoso fingering his strings or using his bow; I set down simple relationships between colors, which are the visual equivalent of musical notes. The paint—not the violin—makes the music. Bass notes are represented by the deep black which covers the walls. Notice how the effect is not one of sadness, however; *au contraire,* my black evokes its opposite, which is light. Higher notes are suggested by the blue velvet in the case and the sea glimpsed through the shutters. The warm color of the violin and the tablecloth at the right balance the coolness of these notes. I hope that, as you contemplate this image, you, too, will be able to hear its music. Let your imagination go and, little by little, the violin will start to sing for you.

Before a sitting, I often say to my models: don't think, let yourselves go blank. Then I give myself the same advice: clear your mind, empty yourself, abandon yourself to the pure contemplation of things. Much like a goldfish, carefree in its bowl, the painter, the model—even the viewer of the painting—should live in the moment, with no other concerns. Painting, you see, is not about intelligence; it should not try to explain, but rather to express a feeling, through color and design. Finally, painting should evoke—and this is my dearest hope, young friend—a sensation of restfulness and well-being in the viewer—like a good armchair!

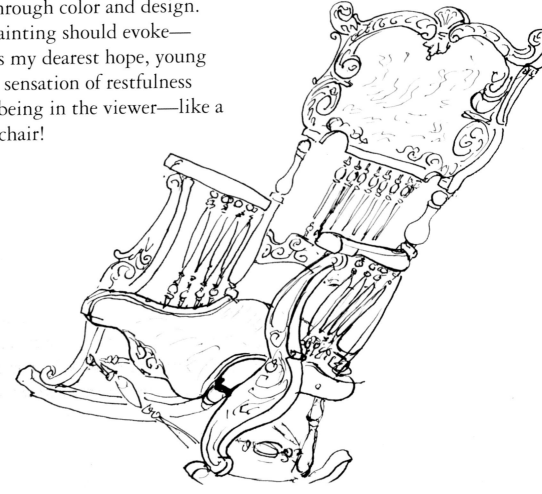

Oh, but don't go thinking that I care only for sleep and silence! A loud clash of cymbals on a scorching afternoon has never displeased me. For that matter, I've always loved the clamor of circuses and carnivals, with the improvisations of the trumpet player, the shouts of the clowns, the rolling of the drums, and the sparkle of sequins in the spotlight. Why, several years ago, I devoted an entire book to the subject; even its title, *Jazz,* suggests joy and dance.

But it's nearly eight o'clock and time for dinner. I have telephoned ahead to the restaurant to reserve a table for us. There, we can talk about tomorrow, Sunday. If what I hear is true, there's a carnival in town. As a reward for being such a good listener, I think I'll take you. If we're lucky, there will be a juggler, a trapeze artist and, perhaps, a knife thrower....You will see how their daring exploits keep the spectators in suspense, holding their breath... Then we could do some target shooting; we'll see if you're as good as I am! I love to try for the bull's eye—it's one of my favorite pastimes. And, as you surely know by now, it's important for a painter to go right to the heart of the matter...

WHERE TO SEE HENRI MATISSE

During his long life as an artist, Matisse created a vast body of work which can be seen today throughout the United States and around the world. Matisse was a great traveler. If you get a chance to do some traveling yourself, you might want to seek out his works in the following places:

UNITED STATES
District of Columbia

Surrounded by gardens on the mall near the U.S. Capitol Building stands the National Gallery of Art. Here you will find *Pianist and Checker Players*, as well as one of Matisse's most ambitious and last works on cut paper, *Large Composition with Masks*, more than thirty feet long. Not far away, in the Phillips Collection, you can see *Interior with an Egyptian Curtain* (page 20), an extraordinary painting with its cool, quiet interior in sharp contrast to the intense explosion of palm fronds outside the window.

New York

Just off Fifth Avenue in midtown Manhattan is the world-famous Museum of Modern Art with its vast collection of works by Matisse. Here you can find his sculptures as well as many well-known paintings, including *The Moroccans* (page 33), *The Red Studio*, *The Dance (first version)*, and *The Piano Lesson*, an intriguing painting of the artist's young son, Pierre, at the piano. Here, too, you can admire some of Matisse's cut paper works, among them *The Swimming Pool* (page 43) and *Souvenir of Oceania*.

If you walk north along Fifth Avenue until you reach 82nd Street you will come to the huge Metropolitan Museum of Art where you can see *Promenade Among the Olive Trees*, *Nude in an Armchair*, and *Nasturtiums and "La Danse."*

Outside of New York City, the Albright-Knox Art Gallery in Buffalo has *Music,* a large and sensuous canvas.

Pennsylvania

If you get the chance to visit Philadelphia, stop in at the Philadelphia Museum of Art and see its wonderful collection, which includes *The Blue Dress* (Page 28), *Interior at Nice,* and *The Moorish Screen* with its richly-patterned surface.

Outside of Philadelphia in the town of Merion is the Barnes Foundation. The Foundation has an impressive collection of paintings by Matisse. While you are there, be sure to see *Bonheur de Vivre,* a fine example of the expressive force of Fauve painting.

Maryland

At the Baltimore Museum of Art, you will find *Blue Nude (Souvenir of Biskra)* and many other important paintings, among them *Seated Odalisque, Left Knee Bent, Ornamental Background,* and *Checkerboard* and *Odalisque with Green Sash,* two of the exotic harem paintings.

Missouri

At the St. Louis Art Museum, you can admire a large Matisse, *Bathers with a Turtle.*

Ohio

The Cleveland Museum of Art has *Interior with Etruscan Vase.*

Illinois

On Michigan Avenue, near Chicago's lakefront, is the Art Institute of Chicago. Here you can see *Bathers by a River* and *Woman Before an Aquarium.*

Michigan

At the Detroit Institute of the Arts you will find *The Window (Interior with Forget-me-nots)*.

Texas

The Museum of Fine Arts, Houston, has the sumptuous painting *Woman in a Purple Coat.*

California

At the San Francisco Museum of Modern Art you can see *Woman with the Hat,* one of Matisse's most important Fauvist paintings.

In southern California, the Los Angeles County Museum of Art has *Tea,* as well as several drawings and sculptures.

FRANCE

If you are lucky enough to go to Paris one day, go straight to the fourth floor of the Centre Georges Pompidou. Here you will find the Musée National d'Art Moderne, with the largest collection of works by Matisse in Europe, including *Violinist at the Window* reproduced on page 15 and the still lifes on pages 24 and 25. Here, too, you will find many of Matisse's cut papers with gouache, among them *Blue Nude II* (page 37), *The Knife Thrower* (page 50), and *The Toboggan* (page 51).

By all means, continue south if you can, to the beautiful Côte d'Azur (the name refers to the blue of the sky and sea along this part of the Mediterranean coast). In Nice, stop in at the delightful Musée Matisse near the Roman baths, where you can admire the artist's sculpture and paintings as well as some of the objects and furniture he treasured, including the famous baroque armchair which appears in several paintings and in the photograph on page 24. And you will certainly not want to miss the Chapel of the Rosary in nearby Vence. Try to get there at eleven o'clock on a sunny morning when the sunlight blazes through the stained-glass windows, flooding the floor with brilliant color.

ENGLAND

Across the English Channel in London, the Tate Gallery has *The Snail,* an exuberant gouache on cut paper. And, at the Fitzwilliam Museum in nearby Cambridge, you will find *Studio Under the Eaves* (page 19).

RUSSIA

If you can travel still further afield, go all the way to Russia, where some of Matisse's greatest masterpieces can be found. At the Hermitage in St. Petersburg, you can see *Harmony in Red* (pages 30 and 31). Also on view are *Dance* (page 12) and its companion piece, *Music,* as well as many other works, some more famous than others. The Pushkin Museum in Moscow houses *Goldfish* (page 49) as well as *The Casbah Gate* and *Zorah on the Terrace* (both on page 34).

IMPORTANT DATES IN THE LIFE OF MATISSE

1869   Henri-Émile-Benoît Matisse is born on December 31st at the home of his maternal grandparents at Le Cateau-Cambrésis in northern France. His father is a prosperous grain merchant, his mother an artistic woman who makes hats and paints on china.

1887   Matisse goes to Paris to study law.

1889   Matisse takes a position as a clerk in a law office in Saint-Quentin, in northern France.

1890   Matisse is confined to his bed after an attack of appendicitis. His mother gives him a paintbox and he begins to paint.

1891   Matisse abandons his legal career to become a painter. He goes to Paris to attend the Ecole des Beaux-Arts, where he studies sculpting as well as painting. Other painters such as Gustave Moreau, Pissarro, and Marquet notice his talent and foresee a brilliant future for him.

1898   Matisse marries Amélie Parayre from Toulouse, France. They travel south to the island of Corsica and then to Saint-Tropez in southern France, to visit his friend, the painter Paul Signac. Matisse brings to his canvases the brilliant colors that will characterize his work for the rest of his life.

1905   Matisse exhibits at the *Salon d'Automne* and prompts a scandal with his powerful and daring use of color. For expressive purposes, faces can now be green, red, or even violet! Matisse is named the leader of a group of painters called "les Fauves," ("wild beasts") whose sole intent was said to be to shock the public. This doesn't shake Matisse's confidence; he continues to go his own way, expressing feeling in his paintings, rather then fact.

1909   Matisse's paintings have begun to sell to great American and Russian collectors. His financial worries over, Matisse moves with his wife and three children to Issy-les-Moulineaux, a Paris suburb. Here he paints *Dance* and *Music* as well as other important works.

1912   Matisse spends the winter in Morocco and comes under the influence of the exotic atmosphere and culture of North Africa.

1917   Matisse moves to Nice in the south of France in December. Although he continues to travel extensively, this will remain his home for the rest of his life.

1930   Matisse travels to Tahiti with a stopover in New York, which fascinates him. He is enchanted with the tall buildings and marvels at the crystalline light which, reflected in the windows of the skyscrapers, makes the skyscrapers seem airy and light. In Tahiti, on the other hand, he quickly becomes bored. It is not until twenty years later that images from his trip to the South Pacific surface and become part of his work.

1931   Matisse accepts a commission from the legendary American collector, Dr. Albert Barnes, to provide a mural decoration for his museum in Merion, Pennsylvania.

1932   Matisse completes *Dance* for Dr. Barnes and continues to paint nudes and still lifes. He also does engravings for books, including a book of poetry by the French poet Stéphane

Mallarmé, and designs the costumes for a ballet, "Red and Black," with music by Shostakovich.

1939   Outbreak of World War II. Matisse moves into an enormous apartment at the Regina Hotel on a hillside above Nice.

1941   Matisse miraculously survives a serious operation. He is cured, although from now on he will spend more and more time confined to his bed and wheelchair. Nonetheless, Matisse speaks of this experience as a rebirth, positive and liberating.

1943   After an air raid on Nice, Matisse moves to Villa Le Rêve in the nearby town of Vence. Here, to ward off insomnia and pain, he undertakes his first works with cut papers to illustrate *Jazz,* a beautiful book published by his old friend, Tériade, in 1947.

1947   Matisse designs the now-famous Chapel of the Rosary at Vence. He creates not only the stained-glass windows and ceramics, but all the furniture and even the priests' vestments.

1948   Matisse discovers that, in spite of ill health, he can still execute decorative works on a monumental scale using his cut paper technique. These works proliferate to such a degree that he must move back to his larger quarters at the Regina Hotel to accommodate them. Approaching his 80th birthday, Matisse continues to work in this technique, creating his last masterpieces: *The Sorrow of the King, The Parakeet and the Mermaid,* and the exceptional *Blue Nudes* series.

1954   Matisse dies on November 3rd and is buried in the cemetery at Cimiez, near Nice.

LIST OF ILLUSTRATIONS

The following is a list of the titles and locations for works of art reproduced in this book. A work's dimensions are given in both inches and centimeters, first by height, then by width.

The abbreviation MNAM stands for Musée National d'Art Moderne.

Cover
Icarus, plate VIII from *Jazz,* by Henri Matisse, published by Editions Tériade, Paris, France, 1947. Pochoir, printed in color, double sheet, $16\frac{5}{8} \times 25\frac{5}{8}$" (42.4 × 65.2 cm). The Museum of Modern Art, New York, the Louis E. Stern Collection (photo © 1993 The Museum of Modern Art, New York).

Page 5
Matisse in garden of publisher Tériade, July 1951. Photograph by Hélène Adant (photo © Centre Georges Pompidou, Paris, France).

Page 6
Self-Portrait with Cigar, 1947. Pen and ink. Private collection (photo Matisse Archives).

Pages 8-9
Illustration by Matei Popovici, Paris, France.

Page 9
Icarus, Plate VIII from *Jazz,* 1947. Screen-print after gouache on paper cut-out, $15\frac{7}{8} \times 10\frac{5}{8}$" (40.5 × 27 cm). MNAM, Centre Georges Pompidou, Paris, France (Museum photo).

Page 10
Top: Pierre Matisse at the Regina Hotel, Nice, 1949, with model for the crucifix he designed for the Chapel at Vence. Photograph by Hélène Adant (photo courtesy Pierre Matisse Gallery, New York). Bottom: *Acrobat,* 1952. Brush and ink, $41\frac{1}{2} \times 29\frac{3}{8}$" (105.5 × 74.5 cm). MNAM, Centre Georges Pompidou, Paris, France (Museum photo).

Page 11
The Dance, 1938, study for "Red and Black." Paper cut-out with pins, $31\frac{1}{16} \times 25\frac{3}{8}$" (80.5 × 64.5 cm). MNAM, Centre Georges Pompidou, Paris, France (Museum photo).

Pages 12–13
Dance (II), 1910. Oil on canvas, $8'5\frac{5}{8}'' \times 12'9\frac{1}{2}''$ (260 × 391 cm). The Hermitage, St. Petersburg, Russia (photo Giraudon).

Page 14
Woman Jumping Rope, 1952. Gouache on paper cut-out, 57¹⁄₁₆ × 38⁹⁄₁₆" (145 × 98 cm). Private collection (photo Matisse Archives).

Page 15
Violinist at the Window, 1918. Oil on canvas, 59¹⁄₁₆ × 38⁹⁄₁₆" (150 × 98 cm). MNAM, Centre Georges Pompidou, Paris, France (photo Philippe Migeat).

Page 16
Five studies of Jackie, 1947. Conté crayon on paper, 20½ × 15¾" (52 × 40 cm). V & VII: MNAM, Centre Georges Pompidou, Paris, France (Museum photo). Other three, private collection.

Page 17
Untitled (Hand with Branch), 1944. Black pencil or charcoal, 16½ × 15¾" (42 × 32 cm). MNAM, Centre Georges Pompidou, Paris, France (Museum photo).

Page 18
Illustration by Matei Popovici, Paris, France.
Inset: *The Sails,* 1952. Gouache on paper cut-out, 28⅜ × 23⅝" (72 × 60 cm). Private collection.

Page 19
Top: *Studio under the Eaves,* 1901–02. Oil on canvas, 21½ × 17½" (55 × 44.5 cm). The Fitzwilliam Museum, Cambridge, England (Museum photo).
Bottom: *English Garden in Nice,* 1919. Oil on cardboard, 13 × 16⅛" (33 × 41 cm). Kunstmuseum, Bern, Switzerland (photo Peter Lauri).

Page 20
Top: Villa Le Rêve in Vence. Photograph by Helmut Nils Loose.
Bottom: *Interior with an Egyptian Curtain,* 1948. Oil on canvas, 45¾ × 35⅛" (116.2 × 89.2 cm). The Phillips Collection, Washington, D.C. (photo Lauros-Giraudon).

Page 21
Matisse in his living room at Villa Le Rêve, c. 1946. Photograph by Hélène Adant (photo © Centre Georges Pompidou, Paris, France).

Page 22
Palm tree at Villa Le Rêve, Vence. Photograph by Hélène Adant (photo © Centre Georges Pompidou, Paris, France).

Page 23
Birdcage in the home of Matisse at 132, Boulevard du Montparnasse, Paris, c. 1934. Photograph by Brassaï (photo © Gilberte Brassaï).

Page 24
Top: The studio at Villa Le Rêve. Photograph by Hélène Adant (photo © Centre Georges Pompidou, Paris, France).
Bottom: *Still Life, Fruits and Chinese Vase,* 1941. Pen and ink on paper, 20½ × 15¾" (52 × 40 cm). MNAM, Centre Georges Pompidou, Paris, France (Museum photo).

Page 25
Still Life with a Magnolia, 1941. Oil on canvas, 29⅛ × 39¾" (74 × 101 cm). MNAM, Centre Georges Pompidou, Paris, France (Museum photo).

Page 26
Interior with Aubergines, 1911. Distemper on canvas, 6'10⅛ × 8'⅞" (212 × 246 cm). Musée de Grenoble, Grenoble, France (photo © Musée de Grenoble, courtesy Andre Morin).

Page 27
Top: *Still Life with a Red Rug,* 1906. Oil on canvas, 35 × 45⅞" (89 × 116.5 cm). Musée de Grenoble, Grenoble, France (photo © Musée de Grenoble, courtesy Andre Morin).
Bottom: Silk carpet, Iran, mid-sixteenth century. Foundation Calouste Gulbenkian, Lisbon, Portugal (photo Skira Archives).

Page 28
Lady in Blue, 1937. Oil on canvas, 36½ × 29" (92.7 × 73.6 cm). Mrs. John Wintersteen Collection, Museum of Art, Philadelphia, Pennsylvania (Museum photo).

Page 29
Woman in an Embroidered Blouse with Necklace, 1936. Pen and ink, 21¼ × 17¾" (54 × 45 cm). The Fogg Art Museum, Harvard University Art Museums, Cambridge, Massachusetts, bequest of Meta and Paul J. Sachs (photo Skira Archives).

Pages 30-31
Harmony in Red, 1908. Oil on canvas, 70⅞ × 6'6¾" (180 × 220 cm). The Hermitage, St. Petersburg, Russia (photo Giraudon).

Page 32
Top: Horse vessel, 2,000 B.C. Painted ceramic. Musée Bastan, Teheran, Iran (photo Skira Archives).
Middle: *St. George and the Dragon,* School of Novgorod, fifteenth century. Egg tempera on wood. Tretiakov Gallery, Moscow, Russia (photo Skira Archives).

Bottom: Ceramic pitcher with handle, Kachan, thirteenth century. Foundation Calouste Gulbenkian, Lisbon, Portugal (photo Skira Archives).

Page 33
The Moroccans, 1916. Oil on canvas, 71⅜ × 9'2" (181.3 × 279.4 cm). The Museum of Modern Art, New York, New York, gift of Mr. and Mrs. Samuel A. Marx (photo Skira Archives).

Page 34
Top: Ceramic plate with blue motif, Suse, ninth century. Musée Bastan, Teheran, Iran (photo Skira Archives).
Bottom left: *The Casbah Gate,* 1912–13. Oil on canvas, 45⅝ × 31½" (116 × 80 cm). The Pushkin Museum, Moscow, Russia (photo Giraudon).
Lower right: *Zorah on the Terrace,* 1912–13. Oil on canvas, 45¼ × 39⅜" (115 × 100 cm). The Pushkin Museum, Moscow, Russia (photo Giraudon).

Page 35
The Mausoleum of Tamerlane, ruler of Samarkand, and his family, early fifteenth century. Uzbekistan, Russia (photo Skira Archives).

Page 36
Matisse cutting painted paper in his studio at the Regina Hotel, Nice, 1953. Photograph by Hélène Adant (photo © Centre Georges Pompidou, Paris, France).

Page 37
Blue Nude II, 1952. Gouache on paper cut-out, 45¾ × 35" (116.2 × 88.9 cm). MNAM, Centre Georges Pompidou, Paris, France (Museum photo).

Page 38
Matisse's apartment in the Regina Hotel, Nice, 1953, with *Women with Monkeys* and *The Swimming Pool.* Photograph by Hélène Adant (photo © Centre Georges Pompidou, Paris, France).

Page 39
The big studio at the Regina Hotel, Nice, with *The Negress* in progress, 1953. Photograph by Hélène Adant (photo © Centre Georges Pompidou, Paris, France).
Inset: The facade of the Regina Hotel, Nice. Photograph by Helmut Nils Loose.

Pages 40-41
The Parakeet and the Mermaid, 1952. Gouache on paper cut-out, 11'11¹¹⁄₁₆" × 25'4⅜" (337 × 773 cm). Stedelijk Museum, Amsterdam, Holland (Museum photo).

Pages 42–43

The Wave, 1952. Gouache on paper cut-out, 20⅛ × 62⅜" (51.1 × 158.5 cm). Musée Matisse, Nice, France (Museum photo).

Page 43

Top: *The Swimming Pool,* 1952. Gouache on paper cut-out on burlap panels, 7'6⅝ × 26'1½" (230.1 × 796.1 cm). The Museum of Modern Art, New York, Mrs. Bernard F. Gimbel Fund (photo Skira Archives).

Pages 44–45

The Chapel of the Rosary at Vence, designed and built by Pierre Matisse and Brother L. B. Rayssiguier, 1947–1951. Photograph by Helmut Nils Loose.

Page 46

The Silence Living in Houses, 1947. Oil on canvas, 24 × 19⅝" (61 × 50 cm). Private collection (photo Matisse Archives).

Page 47

Interior with Violin, 1917-18. Oil on canvas, 45⅝ × 35" (116 x 89 cm). The J. Rump Collection, Statens Museum for Kunst, Copenhagen, Denmark (photo Hans Petersen).

Page 48

Top: *Figure Facing Goldfish Bowl,* 1929. Pen and ink, 47¼ × 56⅝" (120 × 144 cm). Bibliothèque Nationale, Paris, France (photo Bibliothèque Nationale, Paris).
Bottom: *My Rocking Chair in Tahiti,* 1930. Pen and ink. Private collection (photo Skira Archives).

Page 49

Goldfish, 1912. Oil on canvas, 57½ × 38⅛" (146 × 97 cm). The Pushkin Museum, Moscow, Russia (photo Giraudon).

Page 50

The Knife Thrower, Plate XV from *Jazz,* 1947. Screen-print after gouache on paper cut-out, 16⅝ × 25⅝" (42.5 × 65.1 cm). MNAM, Centre Georges Pompidou, Paris, France (Museum photo).

Page 51

The Toboggan, plate XX from *Jazz,* 1947. Screenprint after gouache on paper cut-out, 9⅞ × 10⅝" (25 × 27 cm). MNAM, Centre Georges Pompidou, Paris, France (Museum photo).

First published in the United States of America in 1994 by
Rizzoli International Publications, Inc.
300 Park Avenue South
New York, New York 10010

Library of Congress Cataloging-in-Publication Data

Rodari, Florian.
   [Dimanche avec Matisse. English]
   A Weekend with Matisse / by Florian Rodari; translated by Joan Knight
      p. cm.
   ISBN 0-8478-1792-X
   1. Matisse, Henri, 1869–1954—Juvenile literature. 2 Artists—France—
Biography—Juvenile literature. [1. Matisse, Henri, 1869–1954. 2. Artists.]
I. Matisse, Henri, 1869–1954. II. Title.
N6853.M33R6413 1994
709'.2—dc20
                                       93-41671
                                           CIP
                                             AC

Design by Mary McBride
Printed in Hong Kong